WHO DO YOU SEE WHEN YOU LOOK AT ME?

ANGELA RAY RODGERS

with Grace Anna

BroadStreet
KIDS

Who do you see when you look at me?
Most notice my wheelchair, my voice, or
my crazy hair. But there is more to me
than just what you see.

Some things I do just like you.
I also have talents that make me unique.
When we learn about new people,
great things can happen!

Open your mind and your heart,
and you will see the real me.

"Hey everybody, this is your girl, Grace Anna!"

I love tickles from my big brother. I am his favorite; he thinks I don't know, but I do. When it is time to do our chores, I help put the dishes away.

Yum! I smell something wonderful. Dad is cooking dinner. Mom helps me to the table, and we hold hands to bless the food.

I help, I love, I thank my God above.

I am part of a family.

I brush his soft, fuzzy fur. As he leans in, his whiskers tickle my cheeks. He says hello with a sloppy, wet lick.

I wrap my arms around him for a big hug. He puts his head on my shoulder. I sneak a treat—his favorite snack. He jumps and wags his tail as he gobbles it up.

I water, I feed, I take care of his needs.

I am a pet owner.

A smile spreads across my face as laughter fills the air. My very best friend shines the light, so shadows dance across the ceiling.

Our fingers make fun shapes—animals, trees, and creatures unknown.
"Shhhh." Mom reminds us it is bedtime.
But who can sleep with all this fun?

I whisper, I play, I share my day.

I am a friend.

The bright sun shines in my eyes, making it hard
to see. I hold the bat tightly in my hands and
smack the ball into the sky.

Clouds of dust follow me as I roll to first base.
The fielder throws the ball, trying to make the out.
The crowd cheers louder, hoping I get there in time.

I push, I lean, I make it safe and clean.

I am a teammate.

My pencil glides across the page as I write about my day. I fill the lines with words describing my many adventures.

Adding and subtracting makes my brain dizzy. Sometimes it is hard to keep it straight. I slow down and think, taking time to understand.

I listen, I create, I concentrate.

I am a student.

snuggle

hug

cuddle

embrace

gentle

love

This morning, I expertly baked some delicious cookies with Mom. They were yummy . . .

My friend and I had so much fun!

After lunch, I played basketball.

I push the rock across the wet sand. Something is hiding under it. Look! It's a little critter. I carefully put it in my hand.

I look for clues to solve the mystery. What is it? I dig deeper, searching for answers wherever they may be.

I search, I discover, my world I uncover.

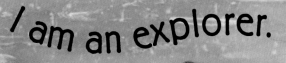
I am an explorer.

I hold the shovel tightly, digging up dirt to make a hole. I rest the plant in the rich soil, and gather the earth around its roots.

I give it a long drink of water, and make sure the sun can shine on it. I have created a safe home for my plant. Soon I will eat delicious red tomatoes.

I water, I hoe, I help my plants grow.

I am a gardener.

The rhythm of the song moves me. Notes escape my mouth, and a beautiful sound fills the air. It brings joy to all who can hear it.

Slowly the song builds. I reach down deep for the very high note. The energy in my soul makes my body tingle.

I perform, I write, my song is bright.

I am a singer.

BOOM! BOOM! BOOM!

I feel the rhythm of the drums. The guitar, piano, and saxophone jump in. The music lightens my worry and tickles my feet.

My body sways gracefully as my hands wave in the air. I feel the song deep in my soul. Side to side, I move with the beat.

I twirl, I pose, I let myself go.

I am a dancer.

The water splashes around me when I kick my legs.
My arms spin like windmills, pushing the water away.

I paddle to the deep end where Dad waits. I need
some help, but I am doing most of it by myself.

I splash, I flip, I do a fancy dip.
I am a swimmer.

BEEP. BEEP. BEEP.

The monitor checks my heart, lungs, and blood. Tubes go in and tubes come out. One more surgery could help me stand.

I am afraid, but in my heart I know I will be okay. I close my eyes, breathe in, and count to ten. When I wake up and look around, Mom is holding my hand.

I need help, I rest, I take a lot of tests.
I am a patient.

GET WELL soon

The platform is full of dazzling light. The atmosphere is electric! Goosebumps dance across my skin, and my heart pounds in my chest.

The moment I dreamed of is finally here. I roll to the microphone and take a deep breath. The song flows from my heart and into the excited crowd.

I hope, I see, I believe it is meant to be.

I am a dreamer.

Although I might seem different, I am a happy girl with much to share. I am a lot like you, and you're a lot like me.

God has given us each a purpose—our own special light that burns bright if we let it. We can all change the world with love and respect for each other.

Now who do you see when you look at me? I'm a little girl who lives as she was created to be.

I am Grace Anna.

About the Author

Angela Ray Rodgers is happily married to her husband, Jeff. They have two amazing children—Isaiah and Grace Anna. Angela has a master's degree in educational leadership and is a former middle school science teacher. On her journey as an advocate for people with intellectual and physical disabilities, she wrote the heartwarming story of her daughter in *Grace Anna Sings*. Angela is part of various programs that help people with disabilities. She and Grace Anna travel the world inspiring others. The Rodgers family lives near Dunnville, Kentucky.

About Grace Anna

Grace Anna Rodgers has a rare form of Dwarfism called Conradi Hunermann Syndrome. The genetic condition has affected many parts of her body including her eyes, ears, skin, hair, lungs, bones, and muscles. She has had over fifteen surgeries and procedures and does physical and occupational therapy to help her function to the best of her ability. She is currently on a journey to learn how to walk. Even though the condition causes her to have short stature, she stands as if she is ten feet tall. She is known for her rendition of the *Star-Spangled Banner* along with other songs she loves. Her bright, bubbly personality inspires others to live life joyfully no matter the circumstance.

Follow me!

graceannasings.org
facebook.com/graceannasings
youtube.com/graceannasings

Contact me!

4graceanna@gmail.com
PO Box 910
Liberty, KY 42539

BroadStreet Publishing® Group, LLC.
Savage, Minnesota, USA
Broadstreetpublishing.com

Who Do You See When You Look at Me?

Illustrated by Janet Samuel.
Photos by BJ Mac Photography. Used with permission.

978-1-4245-5836-0
978-1-4245-5837-7 (ebook)

Design by Chris Garborg | garborgdesign.com
Compiled and edited by Michelle Winger | literallyprecise.com

Printed in China.

19   20   21   22   23   24   25   7   6   5   4   3   2   1